Clownfish

BY KARA L. LAUGHLIN

The Child's World®
childsworld.com

Published by The Child's World®
1980 Lookout Drive • Mankato, MN 56003-1705
800-599-READ • www.childsworld.com

DESIGN ELEMENTS
© creatOR76/Shutterstock.com: porthole
© keren-seg/Shutterstock.com: water

PHOTO CREDITS
© Aleksey Stemmer/Shutterstock.com: 5; cbpix/Shutterstock.com: cover, 1; Ethan Daniels/Shutterstock.com: 17; Hans Gert Broeder/Shutterstock.com: 12-13; Krzysztof Odziomek/Shutterstock.com: 14-15; littlesam/Shutterstock.com: 8-9; magnusdeepbelow/Shutterstock.com: 6-7, 11; optionm/Shutterstock.com: 18-19; Richard Whitcombe/Shutterstock.com: 20-21

ISBN: 9781503816848
LCCN: 2016945652

Printed in the United States of America
PA02326

NOTE FOR PARENTS AND TEACHERS

The Child's World® helps early readers develop their informational-reading skills by providing easy-to-read books that fascinate them and hold their interest. Encourage new readers by following these simple ideas:

BEFORE READING

- Page briefly through the book. Discuss the photos. What does the reader think he or she will learn in this book? Let the child ask questions.
- Look at the glossary together. Discuss the words.

READ THE BOOK

- Now read the book together, or let the child read the book independently.

AFTER READING

- Urge the child to think more. Ask questions such as, "What things are different among the animals shown in this book?"

Contents

Colorful Clownfish

What is that bright fish? It is a clownfish! Clownfish are small. They have white stripes. They live in **coral reefs**. Many kinds of plants and animals live in reefs.

Did you know?

Clownfish are about 4 inches (11 centimeters) long.

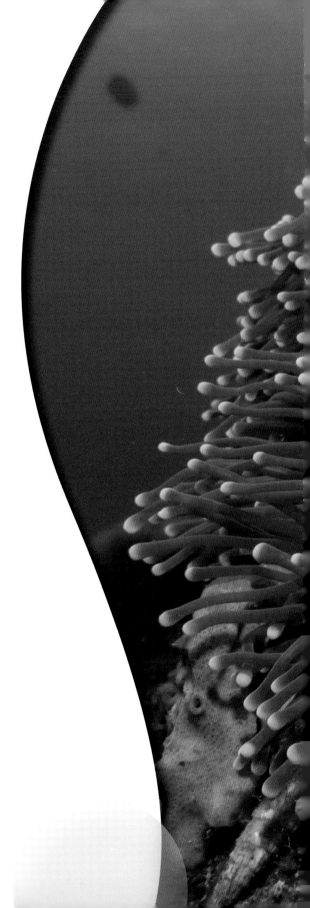

A Home That Stings

Clownfish live in **anemones**. Anemones are sea creatures. They sting. Their sting can kill a fish.

Did you know?

Only 10 kinds of anemones are home to clownfish.

But anemones do not hurt clownfish.
Clownfish have thick **mucus** on
their skin.

Did you know?

People have
mucus, too.
It is what makes
your nose runny.

The slimy mucus keeps clownfish
safe from stings.

Partners

The anemone helps the clownfish. It is a safe home. The clownfish helps the anemone. It cleans the anemone and protects it. Clownfish and anemones work together to stay alive.

Did you know?

Clownfish poop is food for anemones.

Food

Clownfish eat plants and animals. They do not hunt. They eat what they find.

Did you know?

Fish, sharks, and eels eat clownfish.

Did you know?

Once a clownfish is female, it stays female.

A Clownfish Family

Clownfish live in small groups. One female lives with a few males. If the female dies, the biggest male changes. He becomes a female!

Eggs

Female clownfish lay eggs. The males care for the eggs. They wave their fins over them. This keeps the eggs healthy.

Did you know?

Clownfish can lay 1,000 eggs at one time.

In about a week, the eggs hatch. The young are not fish yet. They are **larvae**.

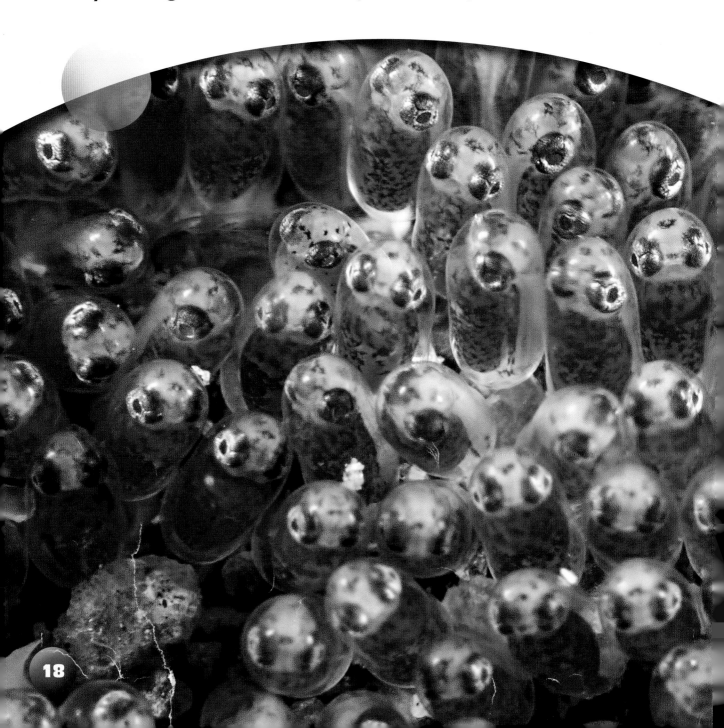

The larvae float away. Each finds an anemone. There, it is safe. It can grow into a fish.

Anemones and clownfish make a good team. They work together to live and grow.

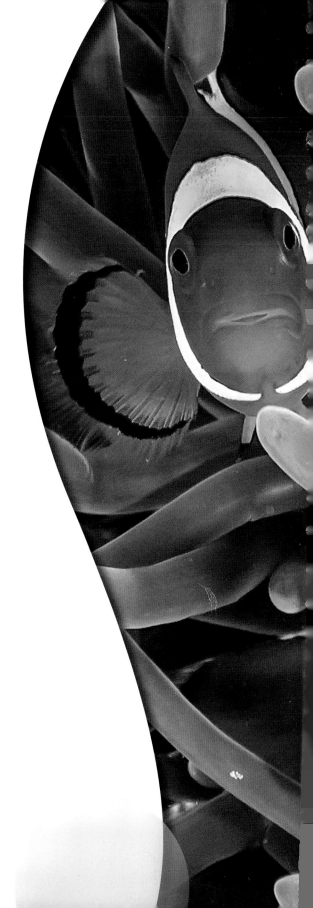

Did you know?

Clownfish live for about 6 years.

GLOSSARY

anemone (uh-NEM-uh-nee): A sea creature with wavy tentacles that sting is an anemone. Clownfish live in anemones.

coral reefs (KOR-ul REEFS): Underwater homes where coral grows are coral reefs. Many types of sea creatures live in reefs.

larvae (LAR-vee): Baby clownfish are born as larvae. They are clear and are only the size of a grain of rice.

mucus (MYOO-kuss): Slime that a body makes is mucus. On clownfish, mucus protects them from anemone stings.

TO LEARN MORE

In the Library

Cunningham, Kevin. *Clownfish and Sea Anemones.*
Ann Arbor, MI: Cherry Lake Publishing, 2016.

Gibbs, Maddie. *Clownfish*. New York, NY: PowerKids Press, 2014.

Meister, Cari. *Clownfish*. Minneapolis, MN: Jump!, 2014.

INDEX

About the Author

Kara L. Laughlin is an artist and writer who lives in Virginia with her husband, three kids, two guinea pigs, and a dog. She is the author of two dozen nonfiction books for kids.